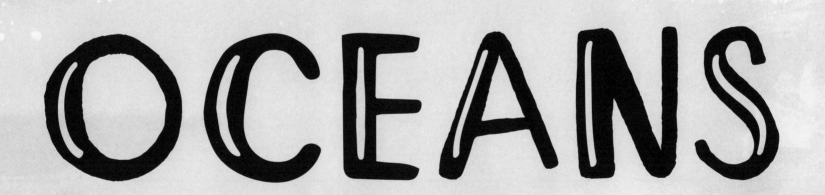

OCEANS

Carron Brown

Illustrated by Becky Thorns

Kane Miller
A DIVISION OF EDC PUBLISHING

Five great oceans ebb and flow over our planet: the Arctic, the Atlantic, the Southern, the Indian, and the Pacific.

These underwater worlds are teeming with wildlife. If you look beneath the waves, through the seaweed, and among the colorful coral, you will see the animals living there.

Shine a flashlight behind the page or hold it to the light to reveal what is hidden, and discover a watery world of great surprises.

The world's smallest and coldest ocean is the Arctic Ocean.

Its waters are mostly covered with ice.

Who is peeking out of this hole?

It's a narwhal. This type of whale uses holes and cracks in the sea ice to pop up for air before diving down again.

Its tusk is really a long tooth, which can grow up to about 10 feet long.

Ringed seals also thrive in this ocean—feasting on fish and using the snow to build shelters.

What's at the end of this tunnel?

A snug, snowy den
with a seal pup inside.

This secret home
under the snow keeps
the pup safe while
its mother hunts.

In Summer, Some of the ice melts and more animals visit the Arctic Ocean waters.

Which animals are swimming here?

Orcas! They travel up from warmer
waters to feed on fish.

These large dolphins
live in a family group
called a pod.

The Atlantic Ocean is the second-largest of Earth's five oceans. Silvery shoals of herring swim in these waters, darting left and right.

What's scaring them?

Whoosh!

Puffins are chasing them.

These birds dive into the water to snap up the herring. One puffin can hold around ten fish in its beak at once.

Some ocean animals spend time on land, as well as in the water.

Who's left tracks on this sandy Atlantic beach?

A group of baby leatherback turtles.

These turtles hatch from eggs in nests under the sand, then crawl to the ocean and swim away. They then return to the same beach every year, to lay their own eggs.

Down in the deep Atlantic Ocean, it's cold and dark, but life can still be found.

This shrimp has spotted a strange light— where is it coming from?

Snap!

An anglerfish
is hunting
using a part of
its body that
can make light.

Animals that swim close to take
a look are gobbled up!

The Southern Ocean surrounds Antarctica.
It's famous for its choppy waters and huge waves.

Emperor penguins,
the largest of all
penguins, dive
for fish here.

Who else is on
the hunt?

A leopard seal is searching for
its next meal! The penguins leap
out of the water to escape.

Leopard seals
are named for
the black spots
on their coats,
which are similar
to leopard spots.

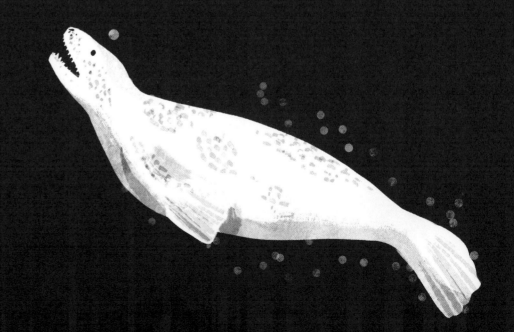

Blue whales often spend the summer feeding on krill (tiny shrimplike animals) in this ocean. These whales are the biggest of all animals on Earth.

what helps keep this huge whale moving?

Thump-thump!

A blue whale's heart pumps blood around its massive body.

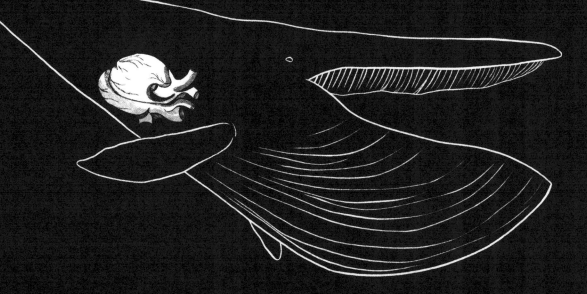

A blue whale's heart is about as heavy as a motorcycle!

At the bottom of the Southern Ocean, strange chimney shapes clutter the floor.

What do they do?

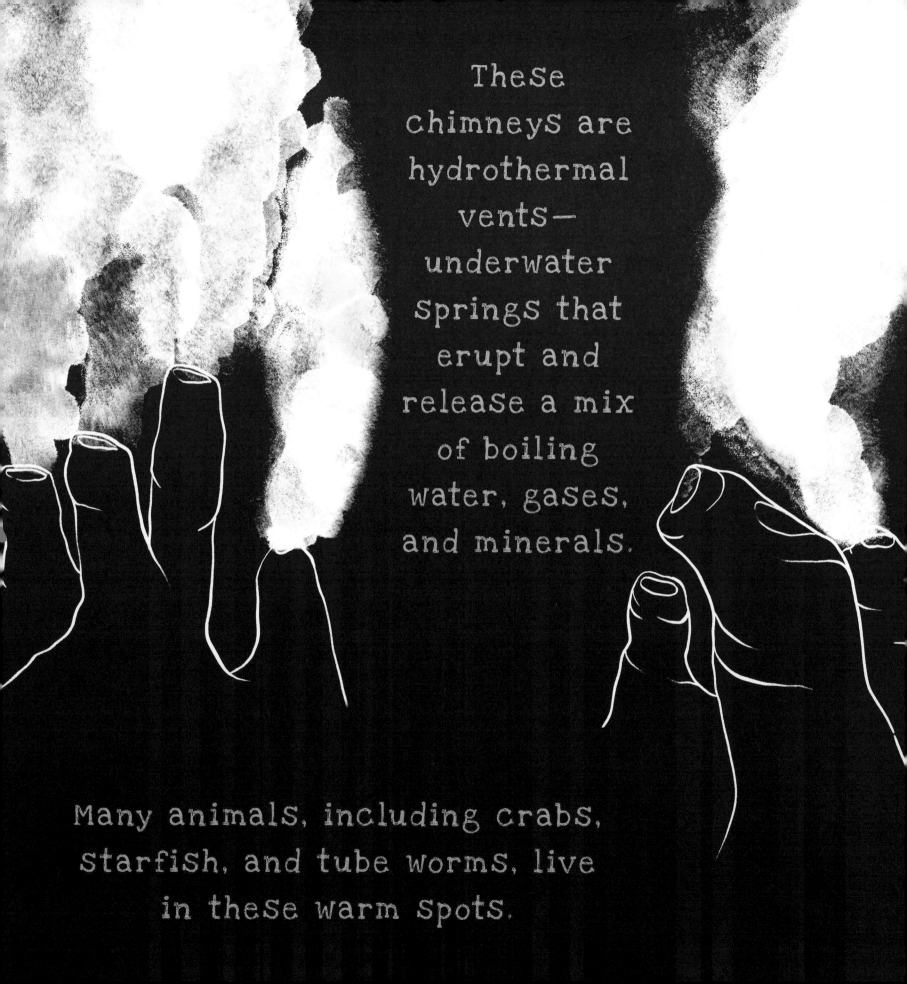

These chimneys are hydrothermal vents—underwater springs that erupt and release a mix of boiling water, gases, and minerals.

Many animals, including crabs, starfish, and tube worms, live in these warm spots.

The Indian Ocean is the warmest of all the oceans, and flows between Africa and Australia.

Many shipwrecks, like this one, can be found here.

Who's hiding inside?

Sand tiger sharks lurk
in the shipwreck.

They are on the
lookout for animals
such as lobsters and
squid to eat with
their spiky teeth.

All kinds of animals live in this ocean.
They often have special features and skills
to help them hunt, or to avoid being hunted!

What has made
this thick,
inky cloud?

It's an octopus.

When in danger, it squirts out ink, then makes a quick getaway while it can't be seen.

There are lots of coral reefs in the Indian Ocean. These colorful habitats attract many creatures, including manta rays.

What's happening here?

The manta ray is being cleaned.

It has traveled to a "cleaning station"
on the reef, where smaller fish eat tiny
animals called parasites that live on the
ray's body, and even in its mouth.

The ray gets
clean, and the
fish get fed.

The Pacific Ocean is
the biggest and deepest
ocean on Earth. It's full of
amazing features, including
seagrass meadows.

Who is taking
shelter here?

Leafy sea dragons are hiding
in the meadow.

These tiny creatures look like plants.
This makes it hard for other animals to
see them and helps keep them safe.

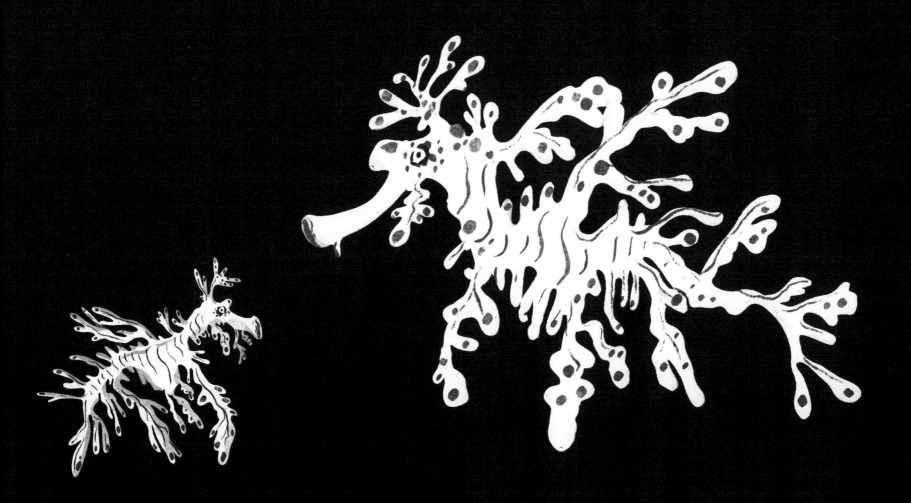

The Great Barrier Reef, the world's largest reef, is in this ocean. The reef is so big, it can be seen from space!

Who is hiding in the coral?

A giant moray eel is lurking—
waiting for a fish to swim by.

Shooting out of its hiding
place, the eel will catch
and eat the fish, using its
sharp, fang-like teeth.

Elsewhere in the Pacific Ocean, beautiful kelp forests reach and sway. Kelp is a fast-growing seaweed.

Sea otters live in these habitats, snacking on sea urchins.

Who else is floating in the fronds?

zap!

Jellyfish drift
through the water.

Their long arms
dangle below their
soft bodies.

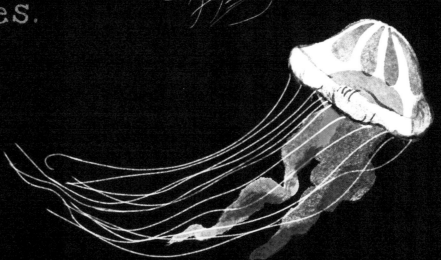

Watch out—the
arms sting.

Oceans bustle with life day and night. Often the wonders are out of sight beneath the waves, but sometimes, animals like these dolphins can be seen above the water.

Keep a lookout—you might
catch a glimpse.

There's more...

Explore the map of the world's five oceans, and learn more about what makes each one special, from wildlife to ocean features.

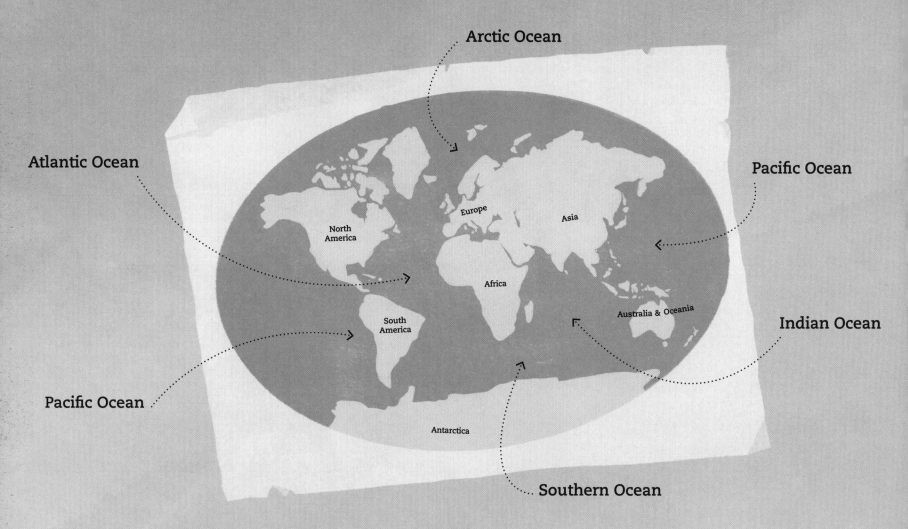

Arctic Ocean

Atlantic Ocean

Pacific Ocean

North America

Europe

Asia

Africa

South America

Australia & Oceania

Indian Ocean

Pacific Ocean

Antarctica

Southern Ocean

Arctic Ocean
The Arctic is the world's smallest, shallowest, and coldest ocean. It flows on the northern shores of three continents—North America, Europe, and Asia. Pale ice covers much of the surface. Polar bears live here, roaming on the ice and swimming in the water in search of food.

Atlantic Ocean

The Atlantic is the second-largest ocean, covering over a quarter of our planet and bordering four continents—North America, South America, Africa, and Europe. Great white sharks, manatees, turtles, tuna, and dolphins all swim in these waters.

Southern Ocean

Surrounding one continent—icy Antarctica—the Southern Ocean is where the Indian, Pacific, and Atlantic oceans come together. The most important food in the Southern Ocean is krill, a small shrimplike animal. It is eaten by whales, penguins, seals, birds, and squid.

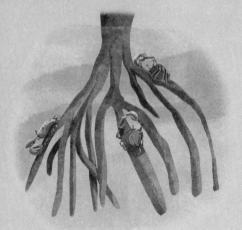

Indian Ocean

The Indian Ocean is the third-largest ocean and the warmest. It borders three continents—Africa, Asia, and Australia—and has coral reef and seagrass habitats. In the western Indian Ocean, mangrove forests grow along the shores of some African countries. These forests grow in the muddy, salty water. Animals, such as crabs and fish, live between the roots.

Pacific Ocean

The Pacific Ocean is the largest ocean, covering more than half the world and bordering four continents—North America, South America, Asia, and Australia. Many volcanoes can be found in this ocean, including Mauna Kea, which is even taller than Mount Everest. Most of this volcano is underwater.

First American Edition 2021
Kane Miller, A Division of EDC Publishing

Copyright © 2021 Quarto Publishing plc

For information contact:
Kane Miller, A Division of EDC Publishing
5402 S 122nd E Ave, Tulsa, OK 74146
www.kanemiller.com
www.myubam.com

Library of Congress Control Number: 2021930481

Printed in Shenzhen, China. PP0721

ISBN: 978-1-68464-288-5

1 2 3 4 5 6 7 8 9 10